REDDITCH
REMEMBERED

REDDITCH
REMEMBERED

ALAN FOXALL

AND

RAY SAUNDERS

Advertiser Redditch

First published in Great Britain in 2003 by
The Breedon Books Publishing Company Limited
Breedon House, 3 The Parker Centre,
Derby, DE21 4SZ.

This paperback edition published in Great Britain in 2013 by DB
Publishing, an imprint of JMD Media Ltd

ISBN 978-1-78091-345-2

Printed and bound in the UK by Copytech (UK) Ltd Peterborough

CONTENTS

Views of Redditch

In *Household Words* (1882) Charles Dickens wrote: "Needles cost human life, at a terrible rate". It never was true, as it is often said to have been, that needlemakers rarely live beyond thirty years of age: but it was, for a long time, true that every needle that was pointed helped to shorten some man's life. The pointers died of consumption in a few years. If the boys tried the work, they were all gone by twenty.

William Avery, who was a Redditch needlemaker and early local historian, wrote in 1887, in *Old Redditch – Being An Early History of the Town (1800-1850)*: I was born at a very early period of my life, of poor but respectable parents, in the small and unfrequented village of Redditch. Though present at the event, I cannot exactly fix the date, but I may say I came in with the nineteenth century.

INTRODUCTION

THIS book has been compiled from the combined archives of Alan Foxall of the Redditch Pictorial History Society, Ray Saunders of R & S Antiques, and the *Redditch Advertiser*, with additional photography by Alan Foxall.

Harry Tarleton's premises on Church Green East in the 1920s, with Gorton's Arch on the left. The shop is now the *Redditch Advertiser* office. The original *Redditch Indicator* shop was on the other side of the arch in William Gorton's old shop at No.11. He was a wholesale and retail ironmonger.

The authors have each produced local history books using their extensive picture collections, bringing into the public domain previously unseen glimpses of Redditch's rich past.

With the wealth of material that is available, a major difficulty in putting this book together has been deciding what shall be left out. As it is not intended that the book shall be a local history text book but primarily a selective history of Redditch in pictures, the quality and interest of the images has been the main concern.

As the Redditch Development Corporation was constituted on 29 May 1964, Redditch New Town is nearing its 40th birthday and so in itself has become part of the town's history and should be recorded.

Until about 1900, although Redditch was internationally renowned for needle making and the associated fishing tackle industry, it was still a small country town but it spawned famous companies such as Herbert Terry & Sons spring makers and the Royal Enfield Cycle and Motor Cycle Company.

In 1827 William Thomas Heming (born 1807) established a flourishing printing business with an office on Prospect Hill and in September of 1859 he launched the town's first newspaper the *Redditch Indicator*.

That was a year which also saw the arrival of the railway to a station in Clive Road and the setting up of the Land and Building Society later renamed the Redditch Benefit Building Society, now the Birmingham Midshires. The paper was published weekly every Saturday (later every Friday) priced at one penny.

Heming had a desire 'to establish a newspaper for the Needle District at a low price and to advocate local interests and record local events and local progress more fully than the county newspapers can allow space for'.

THE REDDITCH INDICATOR CO., LTD.,
General Printers and Manufacturing Stationers.
EASEMORE ROAD, REDDITCH.

The *Redditch Indicator's* Easemore Road premises, newly-built, in 1914.

He was also an agent for the Lancashire Fire and Life Insurance Company and as the town's fire engine was housed in a coach house near the printing works it was convenient for his employees to constitute the fire brigade. Each

W.T. Heming, master printer and owner and founder of the *Redditch Indicator*.

ESTABLISHED—SEPTEMBER, 1859.

THE BEST MEDIUM FOR ADVERTISING !!!

"THE REDDITCH INDICATOR,"

A WEEKLY NEWSPAPER FOR THE NEEDLE REGION,

PUBLISHED EVERY SATURDAY MORNING.

PRICE ONE PENNY !

THE "INDICATOR" has an extensive and well-established circulation in—Alcester, Alvechurch, Astwood Bank, Barnt Green, Beoley, Bentley, Bidford, Cookhill, Coughton, Crabbs Cross, Callow Hill, Feckenham, Foxlydiate, Ham Green, Headless Cross, Henley-in-Arden, Hockley Heath, Hunt End, Inkberrow, Ipsley, Kingsnorton, Mappleborough Green, Rowney Green, Spernall, Studley, Tardebigge, Tanworth, Webheath, and all the surrounding districts ; and is ESPECIALLY VALUABLE AS AN ADVERTISING MEDIUM

ALL OBJECTIONABLE ADVERTISEMENTS EXCLUDED.

SUBSCRIPTIONS :

Unstamped.....................Credit...........Price 5s. per Annum.
Stamped .... ,, ... ,, 7s. 6d. ,,
Single Copies, 1d. ; Stamped, 1½d.

PROPRIETOR AND PUBLISHER,

WILLIAM THOMAS HEMING,

PROSPECT HILL, REDDITCH.

W.T. Heming's *Redditch Indicator* advertisement from the 1879 *Needle District Almanack and Trades Directory*, which was also printed and published by the Indicator Company. The *Directory* was compiled in December 1878. By the time it was published, Mr Heming was dead.

would receive half a crown for his services at the end of each fire.

At W.T. Heming's death in January 1879, Mr Fred Heming became the proprietor. Subsequently the business passed to William Lane.

On 10 July 1975 the first issue of Redditch's first free local newspaper the *Redditch Advertiser* was published from their original office at 20 Church Green East. The fact that local news was obtainable free of charge and delivered through your door soon saw the decline of the existing local paper. The two papers competed for a while but the *Indicator* was eventually incorporated into its rival.

Hopefully this book will help the people of 'old' Redditch relive good memories and evoke talking points and for those new to the town, give them a taste of Redditch as it was when life was lived at a slower pace.

No Longer to be Seen

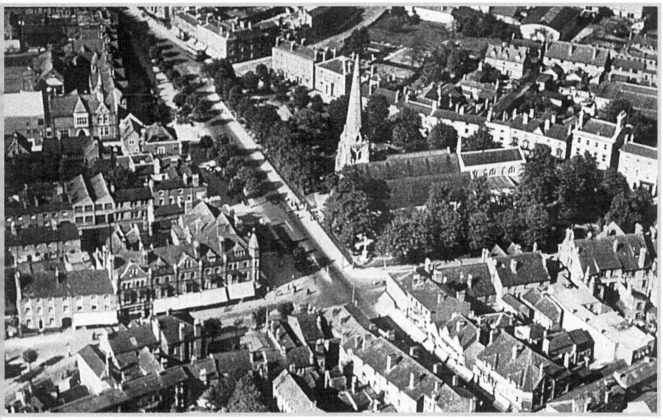

Redditch town centre and Church Green in 1956. The Unicorn Hotel on Unicorn Hill is at the bottom left of the picture.

Evesham Street, in the 1900s.

Evesham Street in about 1905, with Edwin Davis, the licensee of the Vine Inn, standing next to his horse and cart.

A similar view of Evesham Street, except for the passage of about 20 years which has seen the Vine Inn replaced by the Talbot Hotel.

The Talbot Hotel,
30 Evesham Street,
in 1960.

The Fleece Inn,
Evesham Street,
about 1960.

Two
ladies look
into the window
of Clarke's
photographic studios at 47
Evesham Street.

<#>

Evesham Street in the 1930s. The only traffic to be seen are cyclists.

Evesham Street in May 1972. In contrast to the previous photograph the street is jammed with cars.

The Unicorn Hotel, Unicorn Hill, in Victorian times. The name 'Castree' over the bay window refers to Jesse or John Castree, who were licensees in the 1850s and 60s. The tea dealer's shop at the front and the general shape of the building gave it its local name of 'the Cannister'. It was demolished in the 1880s.

The Unicorn Hotel as rebuilt in late Victorian times with the Unicorn Tap on the extreme right separated by the entrance to the yards and stables.

The Unicorn Hotel in its final form as rebuilt in the late 1950s. It was demolished once and for all in the autumn of 1997.

The demolition of the Unicorn in 1997.

The Lamb and Flag, Unicorn Hill, in 1936 when Albert Edward Yates was licensee.

Poole Garage on the right and the view up Alcester Street to St Stephen's Church.

<#>

Alcester Street, Redditch, about 1910.

Two Alcester Street pubs – the Rising Sun and the Nag's Head – both now gone.

<#>

The view down
Alcester Street in
the 1930s.

<#>

The view from Red Lion Street, of the top of Alcester Street and Church Green.

The Red Lion in Red Lion Street, pictured in 1934 when Samuel Atkins, third from the right, was licensee.

The old cottages on Church Green West which were demolished to make way for Smallwood Hospital.

The Parade at its junction with Church Road, the site of the Birmingham Midshires.

Jewell Road in 1905. The only thing remaining today is the road.

A postcard view of Oswald Street, sent on 16 August 1906.

The King's Arms at the junction of Beoley Road and the Holloway before being rebuilt in the early 1900s.

The Rifleman Inn, Park Road, Redditch, all dressed up for the 1953 Coronation.

Smallwoods Row with St Stephen's Church in the background, photographed in the 1920s.

Before the New Town, many Redditch factories were in small back street premises like this one in Wellington Street.

The Jubilee Inn, 15 Edward Street, was just one of a terrace of houses.

Ipsley Mount Nursing Home, near the top of Holloway Lane, was run by the Nursing Association in the early 1920s and later by Nurse Tristram.

Woodrow Farm just prior to its demolition to accommodate part of the Woodrow estate.

The Queen's Head in a leafy Bromsgrove Road about 1910. The pub is still there but the trees have been replaced by houses.

Two children in their Sunday best pose at Batchley Fields before World War One.

Beoley Road was impassible when the Arrow was in flood, which is why the river now has a road bridge.

Redditch police officers pictured in the years before World War One. Sergeant Best is on the extreme left of the back row.

The last remaining toll house in Redditch was at Bordesley Corner. This local landmark was known to all as Granny Lock's Cottage. It has, of course, now been demolished.

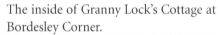

The inside of Granny Lock's Cottage at Bordesley Corner.

The old Park Inn, Evesham Road, Headless Cross, pictured when Jonas and John Wilkinson were the licensees from 1890-98.

The buildings on the left were demolished and area is now The Green.

Headless Cross in 1973 before its redevelopment which involved a main road cutting through the picture from left to right. Here, Mr Drinkwater and Mr Deaves are indicating its position. The old needlemakers' cottages on the right were also demolished and replaced with high-density housing.

TOWN AND AROUND

Evesham Street, Redditch, in the 1960s.

These children are intrigued by the photographer looking down Alcester Street towards Red Lion Street.

The top end of Alcester Street, near the present main Post Office. On the right is Palmer's corn stores.

The Palace Theatre in 1969 before the surrounding buildings were demolished.

The Royal Hotel in Market Place in 1933.

The Parade, Church Green West, about 1920.

Two views of Market Place, Redditch in the 1960s.

St Stephen's
Church and
the top of
Unicorn Hill.

<#>

The old Library on The Parade (Church Green West), previously known as The Institute. Smallwood Hospital is on the right.

The old Library in October 1969.

The Greyhound Inn is just visible in this 1920s view of Smallwood Hospital, immediately above the man sitting on the seat. It was later rebuilt and became part of the hospital.

The top of Unicorn Hill at its junction with Bates Hill. The state of the road indicates heavy traffic between the town and he railway station. The Unicorn Hotel is on the extreme right.

Church Green from the top of Prospect Hill.

The newly-rebuilt Railway Inn (Tavern), Hewell Road, in 1938.

The 'night soil' cart in Beoley Road in 1910.

The man in this picture is John Gibson Blakey who had the contract to lay out the Garden of Remembrance. He lived at 22 Bromsgrove Road, later at The Drive, Beaufort Street, and was sometime head gardener to the Revd Canon Horace Newton who lived at Holmwood.

The Union Club, Easemore Road, in 1909. The club was built in 1893.

A postcard view looking down Other Road. Just below the horse and cart there is now the large traffic island on the Redditch Ringway.

Looking up and down St George's Road from what is now
the Ringway traffic island. The straight section down
towards the church is little changed but the uphill section
was entirely demolished for the Ringway.

From Lodge Farm looking to Studley Road with houses being built in the 1930s.

An idyllic scene at Lodge Pool.

These men are taking a break from haymaking by hand, *c*.1937. They were working in fields to the rear of Easemore Road.

Regulars of the Rose and Crown at Webheath in the early 1930s.

Archaeologists in July 1975 in what was then an annual event – the Bordesley Dig. Now, due to lack of funding, the remains of the rest of the 12th-century Cistercian Abbey lay hidden.

REDDITCH AND THE NEEDLE

Givry Needle Works, Hunt End
1865.

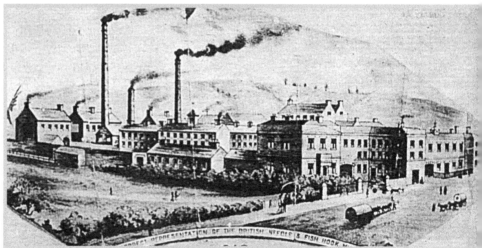

Samuel Thomas & Sons,
British Needle Mills at the
bottom of Fish (Prospect)
Hill, Redditch, in 1840.

Milward's Washford
Mills factory in
Ipsley Street. The
factory was
demolished to make
way for Halfords and
Wickes.

Aerial view of Milward's factory on Ipsley Street in 1930.

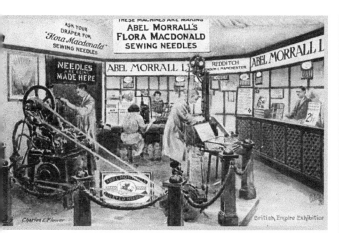

Advertising postcards issued by Redditch needle firms. One of them, from Milward's, is endorsed by Ellen Terry, a showbusiness personality of the late 19th and early 20th centuries.

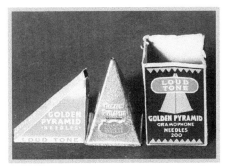

Golden Pyramid gramophone needles were produced by the British Needle Co Ltd at their Argosy Works.

The British Needle Co Ltd sold their Embassy brand gramophone needles in tins of various designs and each style came in Soft, Medium, Loud and Extra Loud, as well as Radiogram.

The Mitrailleuse tubular needle cases contained 50 or 100 needles and could be printed with the name of any company.

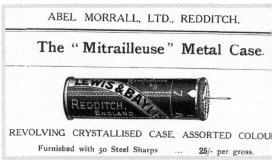

These employees of British Needle at Redditch pose with their long-service awards.

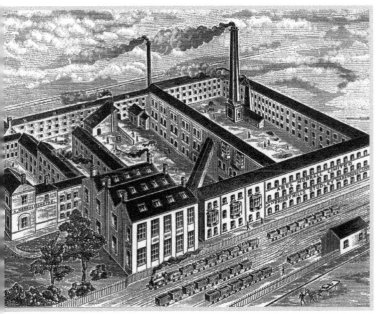

An artist's impression of Abel Morrall's Clive Works at Redditch.

William Woodfield's needle factory in the 1950s. Woodfield's residence, Elmsdale, is top left, set amongst the trees. The railway goods yard is no more but the footbridge in still in use.

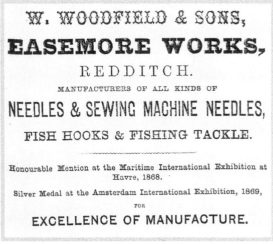

An 1873 advertisement for Woodfield & Sons of Redditch.

A page from Abel Morrall's catalogue showing the interior of the factory in Edwardian times.

Elmsdale, the home of William Woodfield in Elm Road. It was later demolished and replaced by a chapel. The site of Woodfield's needle factory next door is now a driving test centre.

The Old Round House was built in 1799 by William Sheward, a Quaker, who was engaged in the needle trade. It was situated in Mount Pleasant opposite the old Council House. Its original construction was as a wind turbine with long narrow slots in the circular walls, through which the wind would blow and turn the sails of an internal windmill. The idea, however, was a failure and so the central area, which was 28ft in diameter, was divided into four separate dwellings by brick partition walls extending upward through the three storeys. Where these walls met in the centre was the chimney stack for four flues with fireplaces on the ground floor only. This curious arrangement, however, did not provide enough living space and so small external buildings were added later. The building was eventually demolished in 1892. This picture was taken by local photographer John Hensman.

A Fishhook is Just a Bent Needle

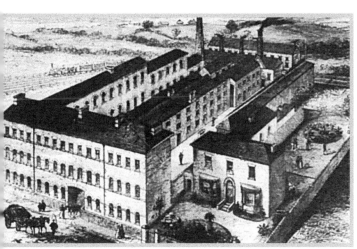

The Standard Works in Clive Road of Samuel Allcock & Co, who made fishing tackle, in the 19th century.

The Allcock family, showing (top left) Polycarp Allcock, (top right) Samuel Allcock at the age of 30, (bottom left) Samuel Allcock in his later years, and (bottom right) Annie Kezia, daughter of Samuel Allcock and wife of J.W. Shrimpton.

The office staff of Samuel Allcock & Co outside their Clive Road Works in the late 1880s.

The funeral hearse of fishing tackle manufacturer Samuel Allcock pictured outside Bates Hill Wesleyan Chapel on 14 October 1910.

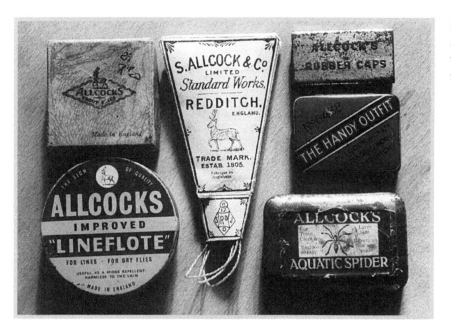

Just a small sample of items from Samuel Allcock's factory. At one time Allcock's was the largest manufacturer of fishing tackle in the world.

Inside Allcock's fishing tackle factory in the early 1950s.

After 37 years of service, one of Allcock's female workers was rewarded with this lapel badge.

In 1950, Allcock's got together the staff who had 50 or more years of continuous service at their Standard Works. Back row (left to right): V.N. Duggins (hook, 1894-1949), A.A. Allcock (reel, 1894-1949), G.F. Dobbins (hook, 1892-1942), H.G. Ledbury (staff, 1898-1949), F. Swann (staff, 1900-1950), T.E. Prescott (staff, 1849-1949), O.R. Robinson (hook, 1885-1942), W.H. Griffin (float, 1879-1933), W.H. Howard (hook, 1895-1949). Middle row: W.H. Griffin (float, 1888-1947), A.E. Fowler (hook, 1889-1949), T.W. Fowler (hook, 1884-1945), Mrs K.E. Brittle (line, 1893-1949), Mrs E. Hands (fly, 1892-1946), Miss F.M. Smith (staff, 1895-1949), Miss E.M. Stubbs (staff, 1899-1949), W. Mayneord (float, 1874-1949), S.W. Browning (hook, 1881-1949), W. Coton (staff, 1890-1946), W.H. Bassett (hook, 1890-1949), W.H. Thornton (bait, 1888-1949), T.J. Boswell (staff, 1897-1949). Front row: Miss L. Richmond (staff, 1895-1949), Miss M. Layton (line, 1898-1949), Mrs B. Robinson (bait, 1889-1941), Mrs F.L. Sutch (bait, 1887-1940), Mrs E.A. Tolley (rod, 1888-1941), Miss L. Evans (hook, 1894-1949), S.A. Shrimpton (director), Mrs A. Bayliss (gut hook, 1882-1949), Mrs H.E. Walker (hook, 1889-1949), Miss F.G. Paddock (staff, 1889-1949), Miss F.S. Birch (gut hook 1894-1949), Mrs L. Westley (hook, 1900-1950).

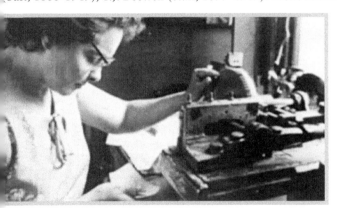

Making fish hooks at Partridge's factory in Mount Pleasant.

Fishing tackle from various Redditch factories.

The packing department of J.W. Young's Mayfield Works in the 1950s. Left to right: Mrs Madge Keyte, Miss E. Mitchell, Mrs Harbon, Mrs Ethel Machin.

Front cover of Albert Smith & Co's 1935 catalogue. Dominion Works was at the bottom of Ludlow Road. The company eventually closed down but their premises still exist.

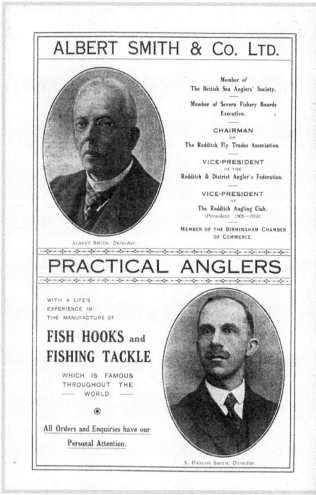

Page from the catalogue showing directors of Albert Smith & Co.

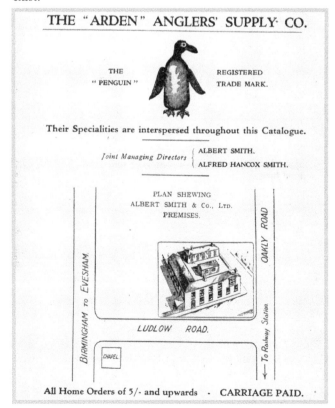

The bait-making shop at Milward's fishing tackle factory at Redditch, c.1914.

This page shows the premises. They look much the same today.

ROYAL ENFIELD

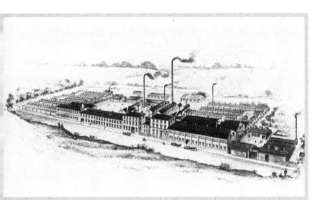

Artist's impression of the Royal Enfield's factory at Hunt End.

A postcard from 1905, advertising a Royal Enfield bicycle.

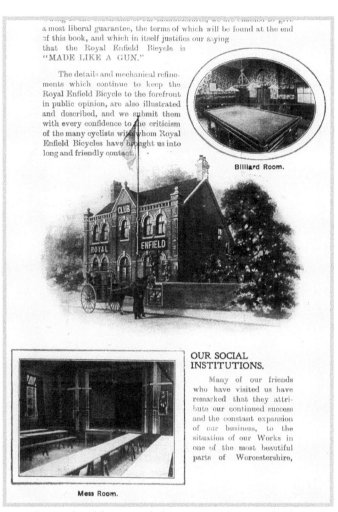

a most liberal guarantee, the terms of which will be found at the end of this book, and which in itself justifies our saying that the Royal Enfield Bicycle is "MADE LIKE A GUN."

The details and mechanical refinements which continue to keep the Royal Enfield Bicycle to the forefront in public opinion, are also illustrated and described, and we submit them with every confidence to the criticism of the many cyclists with whom Royal Enfield Bicycles have brought us into long and friendly contact.

Billiard Room.

Mess Room.

OUR SOCIAL INSTITUTIONS.

Many of our friends who have visited us have remarked that they attribute our continued success and the constant expansion of our business, to the situation of our Works in one of the most beautiful parts of Worcestershire,

Page from a booklet, issued about 1905, showing facilities at the Royal Enfield Club at Crabbs Cross. The building still exists.

Brass token issued by the Enfield Club, Crabbs Cross. The back of the token gives a value of 1½d.

A Royal Enfield workshop in Edwardian times.

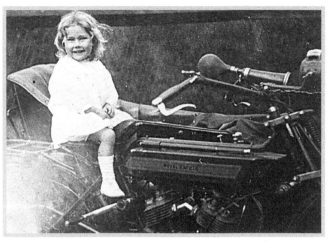

Catching them young… an Enfield enthusiast of tender years.

The Royal Enfield works in the 1950s. At the top of the picture are the coal heaps of Redditch Gas Works and at the bottom centre is Dixon's garage and yard.

The Torrs in Mount Pleasant, home of Harry Lancaster, works manager for Enfield Autocar of Hunt End, who fortunately was not at home when the house caught fire in September 1906. The blaze started in an upstairs storeroom. The fire was tackled by works' brigades from Eadie & Co, the Enfield and the Electricity Works. Mr Lancaster later remarked that more damage had been done by the efforts of the fire brigades than by the fire itself.

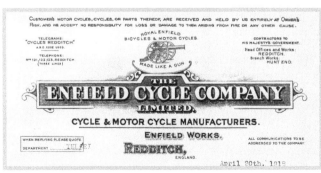

Headed notepaper from the Royal Enfield company of 1918.

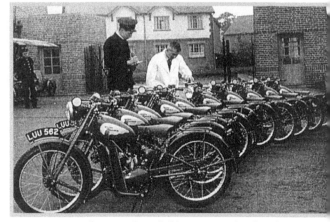

125cc two-stroke Royal Enfield motorcycles for the GPO, lined up near the works entrance.

The ladies of the Enfield accounts department looking at the new in-house magazine *Revs*, in the summer of 1946.

The Royal Enfield Fire Brigade.

The 1951 Royal Enfield staff long service awards presided over by Major F.W. Smith, chairman and managing director, High tea was served by the canteen staff. It must be remembered that food rationing was still very much in force.

Nearest the camera is Royal Enfield technical manager Mr R.A. Wilson-Jones.

Royal Enfield technical manager Mr R.A. Wilson-Jones greeting a visiting dealer from Brisbane, Australia, on the forecourt of the Redditch factory in 1953.

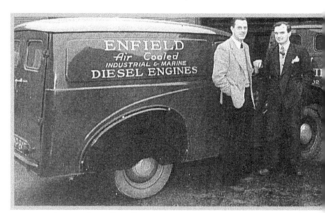

Some of Royal Enfield's transport department fleet of vehicles for the nationwide delivery of cycles, parts etc. These photographs are from the early 1950s.

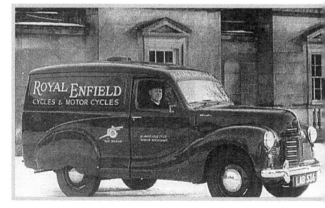

Major F.W. Smith presenting a Royal Enfield bicycle to HRH The Duke of Edinburgh as a gift for Prince Charles at the International Cycle and Motor Cycle Show at Earls Court in 1953.

After World War Two, the Enfield service department was moved into its own new building. The repair department was housed under the same roof.

Royal Enfield motor mowers were first introduced in 1931. In 1951 they are seen here at the British Industries Fair on a stand next to another Redditch company – Herbert Terry & Sons.

If you want your lawns to look their best • • IN HALF the TIME —and without the labour !

Use a Royal Enfield 18" WIDE-CUT Motor Mower. On private lawn or playing-field, the 18" Lightweight will run quietly and smoothly, making 75 cuts per yard.
Foot-started, easily operated and accurately adjustable for height of cut, the 18" model has corrugated land-rollers with full differential action. A Royal Enfield 125 c.c. two-stroke engine, blower cooled, makes handling easy.

Write for Illustrated Folder today

18" LIGHTWEIGHT MODEL

Price: **£60.6.5** Incl. P. T.

Royal Enfield

THE ENFIELD MOTOR MOWER CO., REDDITCH   Props.: The Enfield Cycle Co. Ltd.

1950s advertisement for the Royal Enfield motor mower.

HERBERT TERRY & SONS

Herbert Terry & Sons' head office in 1950.

To cross Millsboro Road from one part of the factory to the other, employees had to obtain one of these brass tallies from the works police.

The 1937 extension to Terry's main works.

Millsboro Road section of Terry's works with the Sports and Social Club at the rear, now a car park.

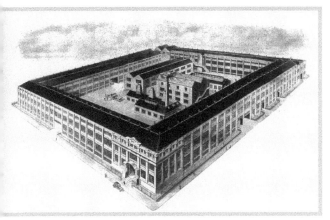

An artist's impression of Terry's main block in the early 1930s, viewed from Ipsley Street.

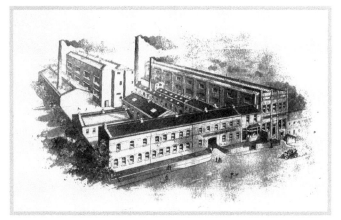

An artist's impression of Herbert Terry & Sons, viewed from the Millsboro Road entrance in 1910.

Herbert Terry & Sons' wonderfully illustrated notepaper from 1914.

Terry's Sports and Social Club in the 1920s. It was demolished in 1992.

Terry's Sports and Social Club interior, early 1930s.

One of Herbert Terry & Sons' trade marks.

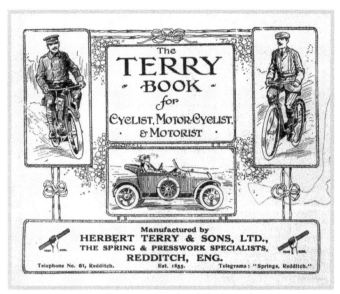

A Terry's parts and accessories booklet issued prior to World War One.

Some of Terry's vast range of products.

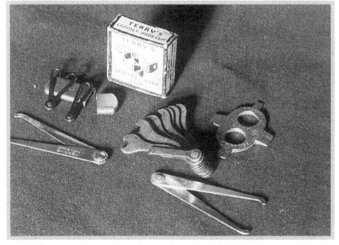

As well as springs, Terry's made a significant amount of small steel pressings such as spanners etc.

Terry's works cricket team, c.1942.

Terry's works football team show off their silverware in 1926-7.

Terry & Sons' Fishing Club dinner at the Talbot Hotel in the 1950s.

THE LODGE ROAD FACTORY

The gate of the Eadie Manufacturing Co's factory in Union Street, built in 1896. The factory was extended in 1905 when it was amalgamated with BSA. Motorcycle manufacture and repair continued there until 1929 when the Batteries took over. These gates and railings are all that remain of the factory.

BSA test riders outside the Lodge Road (Union Street) gatehouse c.1920. The works manager, Dick Nicholls, is standing on the right and second from the left on his own machine is Redditch photographer and BSA rider, Leonard Leyton Sealey.

The gatehouse and 1905 extension, pictured in 1994.

Inside the BSA factory about 1920.

BSA riders testing machines through Beoley Road brook *c.*1920. BSA works manager Dick Nicholls looks on (hands on hips).

Beoley Road brook, *c.*1920, with Webb's baker's green Ford 20HP van being washed. A test rider from the BSA factory in Lodge Road passes by.

BSA Redditch staff football team 1907-08.

Photographed c.1930, the Britannia Batteries' Lodge Road (Union Street) factory. Built in 1896 for Eadie Manufacturing Co, it later belonged to BSA.

Photographed *c*.1930, the Britannia Batteries' Lodge Road (Union Street) factory. This section is the 1905 extension which was built when BSA took over from the Eadie Manufacturing Co. The works police occupied the gatehouse office (the small window by the lamp).

A newly-acquired fleet of delivery vehicles outside the Britannia Batteries' Lodge Road (Union Street) factory, *c*.1930.

An interior view of the Batteries factory showing the furnaces used to turn lead ingots into plates for batteries. Photographed *c.*1930 by local photographer John Hensman.

An interior view of the Batteries factory showing the laboratory. Photographed *c.*1930.

The managing director in the showroom-boardroom of Britannia Batteries.

Works police at the Britannia Batteries Lodge Road (Union Street) factory, *c.*1930.

Fire brigade members at the Britannia Batteries Lodge Road (Union Street) factory, *c*.1930.

The new fleet of Britannia Batteries' delivery vans. Photographed *c*.1930 by local photographer John Hensman on the Birmingham Road, Bordesley, with Granny Lock's Cottage extreme right.

Britannia Batteries' annual dinner at the Talbot Hotel, Evesham Street, Redditch, on Friday, 18 March 1938.

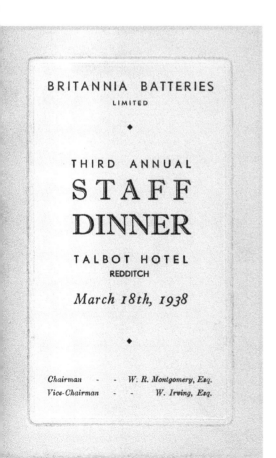

The menu card for the 1938 Batteries staff dinner. It offered Scotch broth, rolled sole, stuffed roast chicken, bread sauce, baked or boiled potatoes, peas, spring cabbage, rolls, cress, cheese and biscuits.

OTHER REDDITCH EMPLOYERS

Power unit production at the BSA factory, Redditch.

The newly-opened BSA factory, Studley Road, Redditch, 1939. Built originally to manufacture the 'Besa' machine gun.

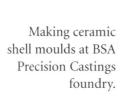

Making ceramic shell moulds at BSA Precision Castings foundry.

Guests at a long service awards dinner for employees at the BSA Studley Road factory.

Fred Hill was just one of the brickmakers working from Ferny Hill brick works in Red Lane (Bromsgrove Road). The business was there in the early 1900s.

The Heath Spring & Notion Company, St George's Works, Headless Cross. Built on the site of William Avery's needle factory, it was demolished several years ago and replaced with a housing development.

Main works frontage on Prospect Hill.

Clarke's branch works in Ipsley Street originally occupied while the new premises were being built.

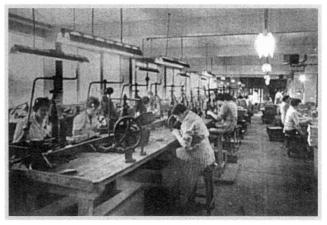

Various departments of Clarke's Sinew works on Prospect Hill in the late 1950s.

Smith & Spencer Ltd Mineral Waters, Ipsley Street, was founded by W.H. Smith in 1850.

In 1907 while W.E. Smith, the son of the founder, was managing director, there was an amalgamation with Phillip Spencer & Sons but this was dissolved in 1913 although the name was retained.

Old enamel shop sign advertising mineral waters produced in their Ipsley Street works by Smith & Spencer Ltd.

Long-serving Smith & Spencer workers. Back row (left to right): H. Jordan (44 years), W. Brown (40 years), T. Woodward (48 years). Front row: H. Ingram (38 years), C.J. Cooper (foreman, 31 years), A. Inglis (foreman, Stratford, 35 years).

A Smith & Spencer water jug would have stood on the ba[r] of many pubs in Redditch.

TRANSPORTS OF DELIGHT

Bell's cycle shop in Market Place in 1905.

Before deciding on your new mount

obtain particulars of

ROYAL ENFIELD

· MADE LIKE A GUN ·

bicycles and motor bicycles.

The 1914 models bristle with improvements and are better value than ever.

Bicycles from £5 : 12 : 6 to £16 : 16 : 0.
Motor Cycles from 41 guineas to 80 guineas.

Inspect the splendid range of models at our Agent's depôt—

**A. BELL,
Market Place,
REDDITCH.**

The same 1914 *Directory* carried Albert Pitts' advertisement offering 'foreign alternatives' of Raleigh and BSA cycles.

Locally-made Royal Enfield cycles were on sale at Bell & Co's music warehouse and cycle agency at 6 Market Place, according to this advertisement in the 1914 *Needle District Almanack and Trades Directory*.

Albert Pitts worked for Royal Enfield for ten years before opening his garage at 50-54 Evesham Street in 1908. The business was expanded in 1915 and again in 1920.

Poole Garage, Poole Place, in the 1920s, at the junction of Alcester Street and Ipsley Street.

The first Redditch-Birmingham bus service on 4 April 1914. The first bus on that service – 09942 – is shown here outside Crabbs Cross Post Office.

The original bus station was where Royal Square used to be.

The 'new' bus station is now only a memory.

A Midland Red bus on the Birmingham-Alcester route about 1920.

Redditch railway station approach and Bromsgrove Road, 1905.

The Midland railway station, Redditch, before World War One.

A busy Redditch railway station in Edwardian days.

A shunter in Redditch railway station in 1959.

Arthur Cole, service manager and chief mechanic at Dixon's Garage in the 1950s.

The Redditch fire engine outside Redditch Garages Ltd, Station Approach, at the bottom of Unicorn Hill, in the 1930s.

Fire crew at Redditch fire station in Red Lion Street in the 1930s.

SHOPPING AROUND

In the 1880s and 90s, No.1 Market Place was occupied by the Victoria Cocoa House, a Temperance Hotel. It opened on 29 March 1880 and closed on 26 February 1897.

An 1892 advertisement for the Victoria Cocoa House.

The Victoria Cocoa House issued these bronze tokens which were exchangeable for one penny's worth of refreshments. About half the tokens that exist have at some time, been 'silvered'.

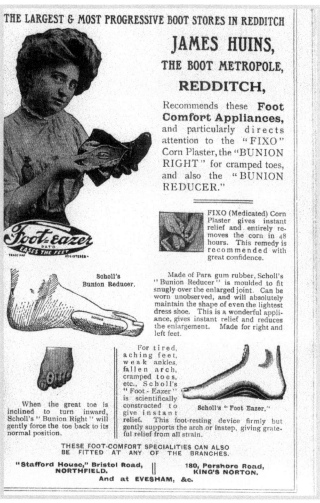

The shop on 'the corner of the town', No.1 Market Place placed this advertisement in 1914.

Piper's Penny Bazaar in Evesham Street c.1922. Note the sheets of music for sale. The manageress was Miss L. Sayle.

In the 1900 *Directory*, boot factor James Huins gives his address as 'Market Place angle'. This postcard was published by E.A. Hodges, stationers, next door at 3 Evesham Street.

<#>

<#>

Hollington's department store on Evesham Street in the 1960s.

The old Redditch Market in 1968. It was between Walford Street and the old bus station. The spire of St Stephen's can be seen over the roof of the Royal Hotel.

The town's busy market place in Royal Square on which has been built Debenham's store. The market, now on the fringe of the Centre, is only a shadow of its former self.

Market Place, Redditch, c.1910.

The Parade, Redditch. For many years Hepworth's the tailors was at the top of Unicorn Hill.

Mr Joseph Duggins and family outside their grocer's shop at 126 Beoley Road, c.1900.

Graham Bennett decorating his father's grocer's shop in Orchard Street in time for the 1953 Coronation.

Albert Henry Lawrence started his boot and shoe business at the Ipsley Green end of Alcester Street in 1910.

Albert Lawrence's 1910 advertisement for his newly-started boot and shoe shop.

Thomas Cresswell's advertisement from the 1888 *Needle District Almanack and Trades Directory*.

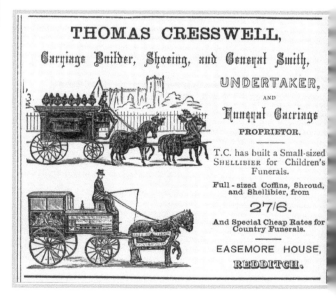

The Redditch Benefit Building Society, Church Green West. This early 1920s building was replaced in the New Town era.

Heaphy's shop at Nos.2 & 4 New Street.

ADVERTISEMENT.

G. HEAPHY,
DRAPER, CLOTHIER, TAILOR, HATTER, &C.

DRAPERY.

CALICOES.	TICKS.	DRESSES.	STAYS.	WINDOW HOLLANDS.
SHIRTINGS.	DRABBETTS.	WINCEYS.	CORSETS.	LACE CURTAINS
FLANNELS.	BLANKETS.	SHAWLS.	UMBRELLAS.	COCOA
SHEETINGS.	QUILTS.	JACKETS.	SKIRTS.	MATTING.
LINENS.	SHEETS.	ULSTERS.	HOSIERY.	CARPETS.
JEANS.	TOWELS.	VELVETEENS.	GLOVES.	OIL BAIZES. CRETONNES.

Black Cashmeres, Alpacas, Persian Cords, &c.

CLOTHING.

Overcoats	Cord Trousers	Mole Jackets	Sleeve Mole Vests
Boy's Suits	Mole Trousers	Cord Jackets	Ditto Cord
Youth's Suits	Tweed ditto	Dust Jackets	Do. Velveteen
Men's Suits	Cord Knickers	Drab Jackets	Ditto Cloth
Mackintoshes	Cloth ditto	Serge Jackets	Pilot Jackets

SUITS TO MEASURE.   SPECIAL ATTENTION GIVEN TO JUVENILE CLOTHING.

OUTFITTING & WOOLLEN.

Brown and Drab Cords.	Merino & Lambswool Shirts
White and Drab Moleskin.	Cotton Under Vests & Pants.
Cheviot and Scotch Tweeds.	Angola and Oxford Shirts.
Black Diagonal Cloth.	Leggings & Leather Gloves.
Ulster and Mantle Cloth.	Tailors' Trimmings.
Cardigan Jackets and Vests.	

Scarfs, Mufflers, Silk Handkerchiefs, Collars, Braces.

HATS AND CAPS.

Boys' and Men's Black Felt Hats.	Silk Hats.
Scotch, Polo, and Velvet Caps.	Soft Felt Hats.
Men's Cloth & Tweed Helmets.	Warehouse Caps.
Boys' Fancy Felt Hats.	Plush and Pilot Caps.

Black, Flexible, and Zephyr HATS in Great Variety.

CLOTHING CLUBS SUPPLIED.

ADDRESS—

3 & 4, NEW STREET, REDDITCH.

George Heaphy's advertisement from the 1884 *Needle District Almanack and Trades Directory*.

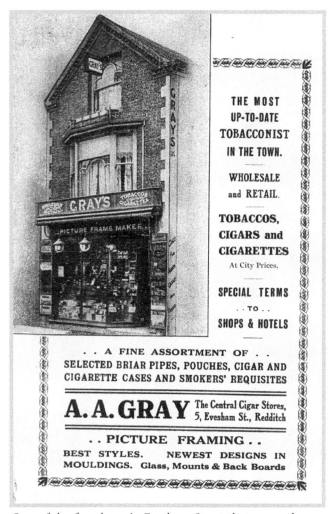

THE MOST UP-TO-DATE TOBACCONIST IN THE TOWN.

WHOLESALE and RETAIL.

TOBACCOS, CIGARS and CIGARETTES

At City Prices,

SPECIAL TERMS .. TO ..

SHOPS & HOTELS

.. A FINE ASSORTMENT OF .. SELECTED BRIAR PIPES, POUCHES, CIGAR AND CIGARETTE CASES AND SMOKERS' REQUISITES

A. A. GRAY The Central Cigar Stores, 5, Evesham St., Redditch.

.. PICTURE FRAMING ..

BEST STYLES.   NEWEST DESIGNS IN MOULDINGS. Glass, Mounts & Back Boards

One of the few shops in Evesham Street that escaped demolition.

Brown's premises at 61 Evesham Street. The archway led to extensive outbuildings and to the old brewery in Walford Street.

Steele's baker's and butcher's advertisement.

Steele's baker's and butcher's shop at 31 Alcester Street, next door to the Rising Sun pub, c.1910. The business was started by Thomas Steele as a baker's shop in the 1880s.

IMPORTANT VISITORS

HRH Princess Margaret's visit to Redditch on Tuesday, 23 October 1962 included a tour of the British Needle factory in Victoria Street.

On 16 February 1973, the Prime Minister, the Rt Hon Edward Heath visited Redditch and met Sir Edward Thompson, first chairman of the Development Corporation.

Prince Philip, the Duke of Edinburgh, officially opened the YMCA complex at the Church Hill Shopping Centre in May 1978.

During the Queen Mother's visit in 1981 she was greeted by parish council chairman Mike Gilbert and his children, Adrian and Vicki.

When the Queen Mother visited Studley in 1981 she was shown copies of the *Redditch Indicator* dating back to 1929, the year she had last visited the town, as the Duchess of York.

The visit of The Queen to Redditch on Tuesday, 5 July 1983.

A wave for *Redditch Advertiser* staff who are waiting at the newspaper's offices in Church Green East.

The Queen accompanied by the Mayor, Councillor Mrs Betty Passingham.

The Queen arrives at Forge Mill museum to be greeted by a member of the museum staff.

THAT'S ENTERTAINMENT

Proprietor & Resident Manager - - - JACK LEUTY
Secretary & Director - - - - IVY C. LEUTY

PALACE THEATRE REDDITCH
Phone: 48

THE PALACE CAFE
(Under the sole control of Mr. Bert Maries)
Weekdays: Open 10 a.m. to 2 p.m., 3.30 p.m. to 10 p.m.
Saturdays: Open All Day from 10 a.m.
Snacks, Coffee, Tea, etc., taken to seats during interval.
Meet Your Friends in the Cafe Before & After the Show

The headquarters of Redditch Carnival in 1956.

A Palace Theatre
programme from 1955.

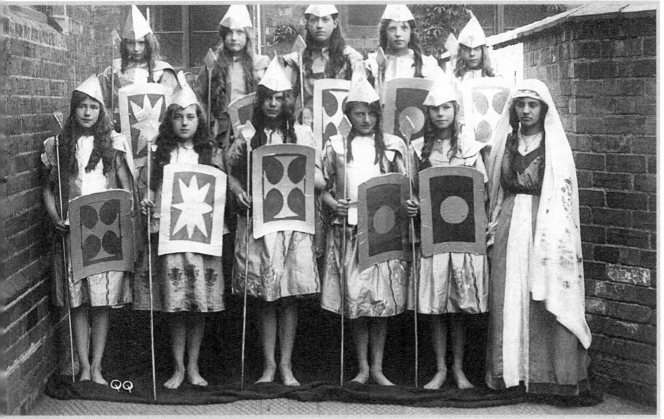

These girls took part in the 1932 Redditch Carnival.

The workforce employed by the builders C.G. Huins & Sons when they built the Palace Theatre which opened on 4 August 1913. The picture was taken by Redditch photographer A.H. Clarke.

<#>

The 1937 Carnival Queen, Jean Smith, meets the matron of Smallwood Hospital, watched by Mrs Wright.

The 1943 Redditch Carnival King and Queen, Arthur Swain and Barbara Lealand, with their attendants.

The 1944 Redditch Carnival Queen, Millicent Phillips, reading her speech.

The 1946 Redditch Carnival Queen, Eileen Mutton, cheers up a young patient at Smallwood Hospital.

A float which took part in the Redditch Red Cross Carnival in the 1950s. Pictured (left to right) are Hazel Treadgold, Mrs Peasgood, Mrs Dixon, Margaret Thompson, Audrey Install, Joan Hadley and Mrs Beryl Hudson.

Redditch and District Young Farmers Club float at the 1950 Redditch Carnival.

Helpers at a hot dog stall at the 1964 Carnival.

Mrs Hadley kicks-
off a comedy
football match at
Redditch in 1969.

<#>

Redditch Carnival badges dating to the 1930s and 40s.

Bertram Mills's Circus en route from the railway station to the fields at the bottom of Beoley Road in 1937. Top: The procession in Market Place. Middle: Going past Milward's factory. Bottom: Passing the Co-op's branch No.9 at the top of Beoley Road, opposite the King's Arms.

Redditch and District Youth Band in the 1970s.

British Needle works football team pictured in April 1913.

Terry's FC, 1919. Back row (left to right): Cund, R. Ladbury, Glover, A. Maries, P. Peak, A. Perks. Middle: Palmer, R. Hack, Davis. Front: R. Pearce, Wilkes, G. Robinson, A. Brown, Hartles.

Standard Works FC, pictured during the 1920-21 football season.

Webheath St Philip's FC, proudly display the shield they won in 1926-27.

Redditch FC, Birmingham Combination champions, 1932-33.

Reynold's Tubes hockey team in the 1951-52 season. Reynold's later became British Aluminium, part of the Tube Investment group.

The golf course pavilion on Plymouth Road, Redditch, c.1910.

A Midland Red motor coach excursion outside the Railway Inn (Golden Cross), Unicorn Hill, in the 1920s.

This ladies charabanc outing leaves the old Queen's Head pub in the 1920s. The pub was demolished and rebuilt in 1935 On the extreme left stands licensee George Henry Glover. In the foreground his son 'Darkie' wears a tablecloth as an apron.

A picture of Eadie Manufacturing Co's sports day on 20 July 1907 in Red Lane (Bromsgrove Road).

The fête held at Foxlydiate House in July 1906, in aid of the NSPCC. The pictures are from a series of postcards published by E.A. Hodges, who had a stationer's shop at No.1 Evesham Street. One event was a tennis match held on the court in the Rose Garden. The man in the white cap is Arthur Bartleet. The other photograph (below) shows Gerald Milward taking part in a bubble blowing competition. John Milward is looking on.

T.C. Clarke's fair at Redditch in 1909.

A Liberal Party demonstration at the Mount, Redditch, on 28 July 1906.

A Labour Party demonstration in Redditch in the 1900s.

A march on Church Green, Redditch, as part of the 1937 Coronation celebrations.

LESSONS LEARNED

The pupils from Miss Bryant's School in 1921. Miss Bryant is sitting on the left. Her father started the school at 1a Park Road in the 1870s. Originally a boys' school, it was called the Upper School in the 1880s and the Grammar School by 1888.

In the 1920s Miss Bryant's School was in Broxwood House, Bromsgrove Road. The building has been derelict for many years.

St Luke's School, Rectory Road, Headless Cross, *c.*1910.

The County Library Service delivering books to St Luke's School, Rectory Road, in 1926.

In 1926 this building in South Street was used by the Redditch District Education Committee as a domestic subjects centre.

A laundry lesson at South Street, using solid cast-iron irons.

A cookery lesson at the South Street centre.

Empire Day 1910 and Mr Maries and his class pose for the camera at Upper Ipsley School.

Upper Ipsley Infants' School at the top of Ipsley Street was built by Huxley's of Astwood Bank and was opened on Monday, 2 November 1896 when about 60 pupils were enrolled.

St Stephen's School, Redditch, *c.*1908.

The third form of Redditch Secondary School in 1927. The two members of staff are 'The Colonel' (Lt-Col A.E. Scothern MA) and Mr J. Reece. The school became the Redditch County High School and moved to new premises in 1932.

The Technical School, Easemore Road. The foundation stone was laid by the Earl of Plymouth in November 1899 and it was opened on 3 October 1900. On 19 September 1904 it housed Redditch Secondary School which, in turn, transferred to the newly-built County High School further down the road on 3 November 1932.

Form 1R of Redditch County High School in 1948. Local author Roy Clews (extreme right of the middle row) has written many novels set in and around Redditch.

The County High School in the late 1930s.

Crabbs Cross School, *c.*1920.

Crabbs Cross School in the mid-1920s. It became the Harry Taylor First School.

Mappleborough Green Schools, 1919.

Tardebigge Infants School, 1920.

Redditch College of Further Education, Archer Road. The building in the foreground was burned down and in 2003 was being rebuilt and enlarged.

The building of the footbridge over Holloway Lane to St Bede's School, c.1970.

PLACES OF WORSHIP

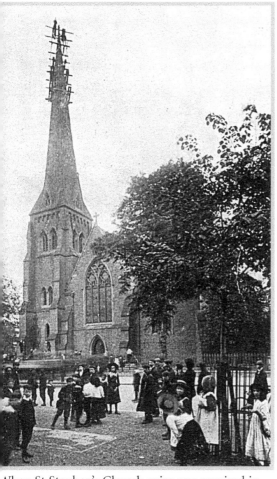

The view looking south in 1905, over the rooftops of Evesham Street.

When St Stephen's Church spire was repaired in 1905, it was done with a few ladders and a minimum of scaffolding.

Looking north to Prospect Hill in 1905.

Looking west over William Street towards Bates Hill Methodist Church in 1905. There is no known view looking east, which of course would face into the sun in the morning.

Gerry Cottrill was involved in repairs to St Stephen's Church spire in the late 1930s. Below him is Church Road with the Midland Red bus garage and the Gaumont cinema.

The view looking south over Evesham Street in the late 1930s.

<#>

Church Road from the spire with the Royal Enfield factory in the distance and the Midland Red bus garage and Gaumont cinema in the foreground. This view is also from the late 1930s.

Another 1930s view from St Stephen's Church spire, looking down Unicorn Hill with the Danilo cinema in the foreground and Abel Morrall's factory in the centre.

In 2001 the 140ft-high spire of St Stephen's Church was almost invisible under its shroud of scaffolding and net enclosure which ensured the safety of workers and passers-by alike.

Local stone, now crumbling, was used to build St Stephen's Church in the 1850s. The new work used a more robust stone from Staffordshire.

Repairs to the spire of St Stephen's Church cost £300,000 from January 2001 to April 2002. The work was carried out by Nimbus Ltd of Somerset, and Northfield-based Conway Stonemasonry.

Compare this with the 1905 and late 1930s view – looking south over the remains of Evesham Street on 2001.

Looking north to Prospect Hill in 2001.

This is Williams Street pictured from St Stephen's Church spire in 2001.

Interior of the Congregational Church in Evesham Street, in November 1908.

The Congregational Church in Evesham Street.

Bates Hill Wesleyan Methodist Chapel and interior, demolished to make way for an electrical goods store.

Member of the Congregational Church Sunday School's senior department, pictured on 1 October 1933. Mr Heaphy, a local men's outfitters, is second from the left of the middle row. Jack Baker, a butcher, is third of left on the same row.

Headless Cross Wesleyan Methodist Chapel was destroyed during a gale on Sunday, 24 March 1895.

The methodist chapel was rebuilt in 1897 with its landmark openwork tower. In 2003 it is due to be destroyed again, this time by the hand of man.

The Primitive
Methodist Chapel,
Ipsley Green, in
1911. There has
been much
alteration to the
front of this
building.

Primitive Methodist juniors, 1910.

The Convent of St Louis Chapel was accommodated in a house called The Poplars in Beoley Road and was listed under Private Schools in the 1918 *Directory*. The owner was Mrs Bryan.

The Vicarage at the bottom of Plymouth Road, Redditch, belonged to St Stephen's Church.

Workers rest from building the Gospel Hall, Evesham Street, Redditch. It was completed in March 1922.

Sunday School treat at the Gospel Hall, Evesham Street, Redditch.

Band of Hope march in 1908, passing Joseph Andrew & Sons, gas, water and electrical engineers' premises on Church Green East.

Temperance festival on Front Hill, Evesham Street, in 1907.

Temperance procession in Church Green East, 21 May 1909.

Redditch firemen are on church parade on 12 June 1910.

Methodist Temperance march, Church Green East, in the 1920s.

New Town, New Redditch

The exterior and interior of Holmwood when it became a convalescent home for the RAOB (the 'Buffs') in 1923. The Revd Canon Horace Newton MA was made Vicar of St Stephen's Church, Redditch, in January 1892. He was very wealthy and built Holmwood as his residence. He continued to live there after his retirement in 1905.

The opening of Holmwood as an RAOB convalescent home by the Earl of Plymouth on 6 August 1923.

Enamel badge commemorating the opening of Holmwood as an RAOB convalescent home.

The extension to Holmwood used as offices by Redditch Development Corporation.

Mr Anthony Greenwood, Minister for Housing and Local Government, talking to some of the first Redditch New Town residents at Wishaw in February 1968.

Redditch Development Corporation's housing office was at No.4 Unicorn Hill in 1973.

Part of the Henley Highway at Watery Lane under construction in 1969.

Construction of the Alvechurch Highway and the pedestrian subway near Lodge Road in the 1970s.

In April 1971, work was in progress on the first phase of the new town centre. In the distance is part of Park Road and Littleworth.

In April 1979 Bovis Construction Ltd started work on the Owen Owen superstore. It is now owned by Allders Ltd.

CRABBS CROSS AND HUNT END

This postcard view was entitled Jubilee Road Estate, Crabbs Cross. Nowadays it is known as Jubilee Avenue in Headless Cross.

Evesham Road and the post office in Crabbs Cross.

The Royal Oak on Evesham Road, Crabbs Cross, is now a private residence with a front garden.

The Star and Garter at Crabbs Cross is still very much in business, although much altered. The surrounding buildings are no more and the approach is different.

Crabbs Cross in 1905, looking from the top of the Slough towards the post office.

St Peter's CC members in the summer of 1926.

Looking down Littlewoods to Hunt End, c.1915.

<#>

Hunt End
showing the
Enfield works,
*c.*1910.

Ox roast at the Red Lion, Hunt End, on 3 August 1909.

Walkwood Road, Hunt End, Crabbs Cross. The house nearest the camera on the left of the picture appears to be for sale.

Astwood Bank, Feckenham and Cookhill

Astwood Bank pictured in summertime early in the 20th century.

Marchers at a Wesleyan treat at Astwood Bank in 1908.

St Matthais and St George Church was extended in 1911, virtually doubling its size.

Edwardian scene at New Road, Astwood Bank.

George Hollington of Yew Tree House, Astwood Bank. He retired from fox hunting in April 1905, after his 74th season.

A gathering of the Harris family at Dark Lane, Astwood Bank, in the early 1900s.

The Harris family of Astwood Bank, owners of the local garage.

The Woodman Inn, Evesham Road, Astwood Bank. The name over the door is that of Henry Walker who was licensee from 1903 to 1921.

The White Lion Hotel, where Daniel Dibble was licensee from 1904 to 1914. The hotel offered stabling and good accommodation for cyclists, billiards and bagatelle, Flower's bottled ales and stouts, and catered for large or small parties.

John Boreham's shop in Feckenham Road, Astwood Bank, in the 1930s.

The Crown Hotel, Feckenham Road, Astwood Bank, c.1910.

Local policeman PC Woods leads a Coronation parade at Astwood Bank in June 1953.

Astwood Bank Operatic Society put on *The Wreck of the Argosy* on 15 March 1918.

The male cast from Astwood Bank Operatic Society's *The Wreck of the Argosy*.

The successful Astwood Bank FC, 1922-23, pictured with their trophies.

Cookhill Priory was for many years the home of the Antrobus family.

Elmleigh, Cookhill, was for many years the local post office.

The Lygon Arms and the village smithy with blacksmith George Newman outside in 1913.

High Street, Feckenham, in the 1960s.

High Street, Feckenham, in the 1950s, showing the Eight Bells.

The Schoolhouse, Feckenham, on a postcard posted in September 1909.

Barrett's of Feckenham, the first shop in the area. They are still there, although the site is now somewhat different.

The Yew Tree Inn, Alcester Road, Feckenham, in the 1920s when Percy Briney was the licensee. He also described himself as a 'haycutter'. No longer licenced premises, it still exists as a private house, hiding behind the yew tree that gave the pub its name.

Another view of the Yew Tree Inn Feckenham

Foxlydiate, Bentley, Hewell and Tardebigge

The Brook Inn, Elcock's (or Elcott's) Brook on a postcard sent on 5 August 1919.

The Fox and Goose, Foxlydiate, projecting into the main road to Bromsgrove. This contributed to its eventual demolition in 1947.

Another view of the Fox and Goose, Foxlydiate.

The bar of the Fox and Goose at Foxlydiate in the 1930s.

Foxlydiate House, demolished in 1938 to make way for the Foxlydiate Hotel.

Bentley Manor, Upper Bentley, in 1913. It was demolished in 1955. It was the home of the Hemming family of needlemakers.

The main entrance to Bentley Manor.

The stables at Bentley Manor.

The Squire of Bentley, Mrs Cheape, in 1918, shortly before her death. She is buried in Scotland beside her husband.

Stained glass memorial to Daisy Cheape in Lower Bentley Church.

Mrs Cheape with the Bentley Harriers pack of hounds beneath the 300-year-old nut tree in the grounds of Bentley Manor. Tom Carr senior is on the right of this picture from 1905.

The Squire of Bentley's daughters, Maudie, who went on to write her mother's biography, *The Squire of Bentley*, and Helen Margaret, known as Daisy, who was drowned off the Isle of Mull in 1896. Maudie is seated astride the horse, called Jenny.

Norgrove Mill, seen here in the 1950s, stands below a lake in front of Norgrove Court. It is now a private residence.

Norgrove Court was the home farm for Bentley Manor.

Bentley Smithy in 1910.

Plaque erected on a brick plinth by the side of Top Lock on the Tardebigge Canal to commemorate the founding o the Inland Waterways Association. A medal was also issued.

The Revd Charles Allan Dickens, vicar of Tardebigge, 1855-1917.

Canal and church at Tardebigge

Artist's impression of Hewell Grange, the seat of the Rt Hon Baron Windsor of Stanwell. It was built between 1884 and 1891.

Hewell Grange pictured in 1906.

Hewell Grange gatehouses, the original entrance.

Hewell Grange gardens with the Old Hall on the left and the stepped grass bank leading up to the water tower which can be seen from the old Redditch-Bromsgrove road.

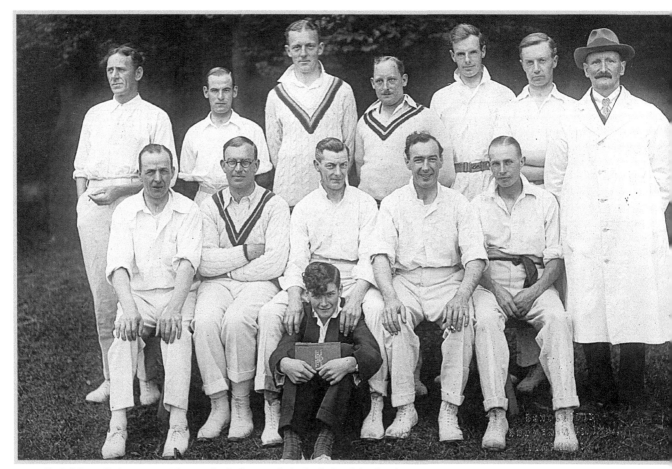

Hewell Cricket Club *c.*1920. The Earl of Plymouth is far left of the back row.

Studley, Mappleborough Green and Beoley

Studley and Astwood Bank Station. Only part of the buildings survive.

Fleece Hill, Studley, in the early 1920s.

Ye Olde Barley Mow at Studley.

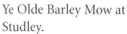

Priory Square, Studley.

Alcester Road, Studley, in the 1960s.

Alcester Road, Studley, looking towards the Duke of Marlbrough in the 1960s.

Alcester Road, Studley, during World War One.

Alcester Road, Studley, in the 1960s.

The Bell Brewery at Studley before World War One.

Flower's beer dray descending Node Hill, Studley, in the 1950s.

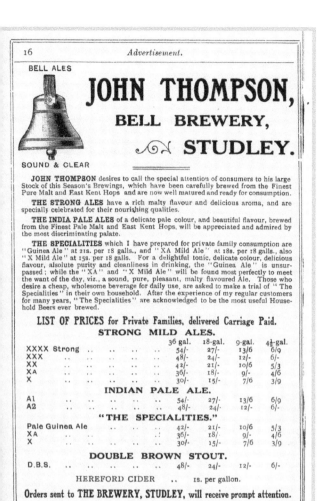

A 1914 advertisement and price list issued by John Thompson of the Bell Inn, Studley.

Old Castle, Studley.

Studley Castle Horticultural College for Women in 1910.

Instruction at Studley Castle Horticultural College for Women in 1910.

The Boot Inn, Mappleborough Green.

Mappleborough Stores and Tea Gardens, later demolished and rebuilt as a private residence.

Mappleborough police station and new cottages.

This 1914 advertisement shows that heavy industry reached even rural Mappleborough Green.

Mappleborough Wesleyan Chapel.

Beoley Mills, Redditch.

Paper mill at Beoley.

Beoley Hall is now divided into apartments.

Start of a race at Beoley flower show in 1906.

The Village Inn, Beoley, *c*.1930. It was also a Midland Red parcel agency.

Beoley post office.

Miss Edith Emms, grocer and
postmistress at Holt End, *c*.1905.

ND - #0368 - 270225 - C0 - 297/210/10 - PB - 9781780913452 - Gloss Lamination